„Read and Play" kann im Zusammenhang mit jedem Lehrwerk im Laufe des ersten Lernjahres eingesetzt werden. Die Unit-Angaben beziehen sich auf „Learning English – Modern Course 1" (Klettbuch 5121), mit dem die Vokabeln und Strukturen übereinstimmen. „Read and Play" ist ganz im Present Tense (Simple and Continuous) gehalten. Neue Wörter sind durch Kursivdruck gekennzeichnet und werden am Ende des Buches erklärt.

D1724805

Contents

"Hello!
My name's
Fred *Brown*.

This is my family:
my father and my mother,
my sister *Peggy* and
my brother, *Steve*.

This is my house ...

... and this is my *street*.
My *address* is
11, *Bush Street, Wembley*."

PEGGY
IS
LATE

Teacher: Good morning, boys and girls.
I'm *Miss Brown*.
I'm your new teacher.
Class: Good morning, Miss Brown.
Teacher: Now *tell me* your names, please.

John: I'm John *Baker*.
Anne: My name's Anne Smith.
Teacher: And what's your name?
Betty: My name's Betty Kent.

Chris: And I'm Chris White.
Please, Miss Brown,
Peggy isn't here.
Teacher: Where is she? Is she late?
Class: Ah, here she is.
Peggy: I'm sorry I'm late, Miss.
Teacher: What's your name?
Peggy: Peggy. Peggy Brown.
Teacher: You're late, Peggy.
Peggy: Yes, I'm sorry, Miss …
oh, what's your name?
Class: MISS BROWN!

3

It is *break*. But the boys are not playing, they are working.
"What are you doing, Fred?"
"I'm learning English. We've got English today."

Here is Anne. She is reading. But she is not reading English.
"What are you reading, Anne?"
"I'm reading a *comic*. Now sssssh."

"Hello, John. What's Chris doing?"
"He's playing football with Peter."
"Are they good?"
"Oh yes, they are!"

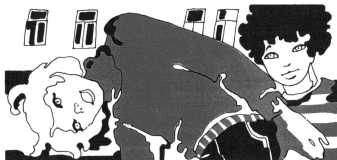

"Here's John again. And who's this?"
"Hello, it's me!"
"Who are you?"
"I'm Fred."
"Oh, hello, Fred! What are you doing?"
"I'm looking at YOU!"

WHAT IS
IN THE VAN?

a table

a _____

5

bedroom

bathroom

living-room

kitchen

It is moving day. *Bob* and Anne are in the new house. The van is gone.

Bob, where's the cupboard?	It's in the ....
And where are the chairs?	They're in the ....
Where's the box with the clothes in it?	It's in the ....
Where's the table?	It's in the ....
Where's the sofa?	It's in the ....
Where are the books?	They're in the ....
Where's the lamp?	It's in the ....
Where are the beds?	They're in the ....
Where are the cups?	They're in the ....
Where's Toby's basket?	It's in the ....
And where's Toby?	He's not here. Is he still in the van?
Oh dear! ...	

6

It is Monday morning.
Fred is in bed.
The alarm clock is ringing.
It is half past seven.
"Fred!"
"Yes, Mum?"
"It's half past seven."

Fred is still in bed.
It is eight o'clock.
Fred's mother is in the
kitchen now.
"Fred! Are you *up?*"
"No, but…"
"Hurry up!"

Fred is still in bed.
It is a quarter past eight.
"Fred, are you ready now?"
"No, but …"
Fred's mother is coming
into his room.
"Fred, you're still in bed!"

It is half past eight.
Fred is *putting on* his clothes.
There is *no time to* wash.
"Where's my breakfast,
Mum?"
"There's *no time for*
breakfast now.
It's time to go to school."
"O-o-oh!"

TIME FOR HOBBIES

Peter's *hobby* is *swimming*.
He can swim like a fish.

Anne's hobby is *collecting* records.
Here she is listening to a folk-song record.

John *likes* tennis. He has got three tennis *rackets*. Today he is playing against his friend Tom.

Betty's hobby is cooking.
She has cooking lessons at school.
Now she is cooking lunch at home.

Fred and his friends are playing football. It is their hobby.

Here Chris is playing the trumpet.
He has lessons and he is a very good trumpet-player.
But he must work *hard* for his hobby.

Today Fred and his friends are having a *swimming* lesson.

Here is Fred.
He is a good swimmer.

Here is Tom.
He is a good swimmer, too.

And here is Chris.
Is he a good swimmer?

Here is the teacher with his class.

But the teacher cannot *see* Chris. Where is he?

Ah, here he is!
He is in the *water*, too.

IT IS LUNCH-TIME

Peggy and the other girls and boys are having lunch at school.

Peggy: Hurry up, Betty.
Betty: Why?
Peggy: It's lunch-time. I'm hungry.

Fred: Oh, fish – that's good.
John: And *chips* – wonderful!
Peter: Can I have your fish?
John: No, you can't.
Peter: Why not?
John: Because it's my fish.
Betty: This is good, mmm!
Susan: No, it isn't.
Betty: Yes, it is.

Peggy: Betty's *right*. It is good.
It's a wonderful lunch today.
Anne: Can I have your fish?
Susan: Yes, you can, but you must give me your chips.
Anne: O.K. Here you are.
Betty: Now look at that: Anne's eating two pieces of fish and Susan's only got chips. What a funny lunch!

AT THE AIRPORT

Fred and Peggy are at London Airport. They are *waiting for* their father. He is coming back from New York today.

They are listening to the loudspeaker, but they can't *understand* it.
It is like one word.
Can you say when their father's plane is landing?

...sengersforLufthansaflightfiveninetwo...

...enthreefromNewYorkisnowlanding

11

THE JAZZ GROUP

Tom plays the saxophone. He cannot play at home.

Peter plays the guitar. He cannot play at home.

Chris plays the trumpet. He cannot play at home.

Tom, Peter and Chris are friends.

Now they can play *everywhere*.

nothing to declare ▶

atoc tah
2 airps fo ssoke
12 dolg chaetws
pam-sajy

a boko
a pari fo serstrou
furo eexrseicl
tow kobos
ollupervs
rouf hirsts

rina-taoc
otw lossube

rdses
wot sriths

ajekct
a raip fo sohse
heert ssrith
kocss
yapjma

AT KENNEDY AIRPORT, NEW YORK

There are some people in the customs hall. They have got suitcases and bags. What is in their suitcases and bags? Who is the smuggler?

13

WHERE IS MY CAR?

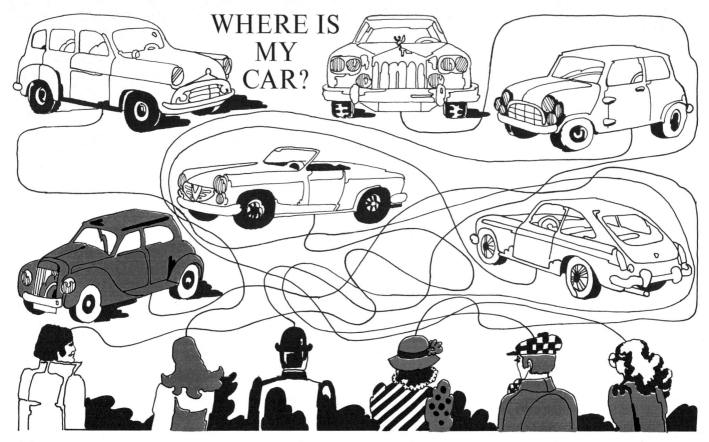

Mr Kent has got
a blue car.
He is looking for it.
Where is it?
14 *Colour* it blue.

Mrs White has got
a yellow car.
She is looking
for it. Where is it?
Colour it yellow.

Peter Simpson
has got a black car.
He is looking for it.
Where is it?
Colour it black.

Jennifer Brown
has got a red car.
She is looking
for it. She can see it
over there.

John Marshall
has got a green car.
He is looking for
it. Where is it?
Colour it green.

Mrs Turner has
got a brown car.
She is looking
for it. Where is it?
Colour it brown.

Spring is a wonderful season. In April and May the days are warm and *sunny*. We can play in the garden and walk in the park.

In summer the weather is hot and the days are long. There are school *holidays* in July and August. We often have lunch or tea in the garden, and we can swim and lie in the sun.

SPRING

SUMMER

THE FOUR SEASONS

WINTER

AUTUMN

School begins again in September. The holidays are over and summer is over, too. It is autumn. The weather is cool and it often rains.

Winter is a wonderful season, too. In December it's *Christmas*. And in January it often snows. Then it is very cold, but we can play in the snow and make *snowmen*.

15

Tom & Henry

There's a *snowman* over there, Tom.

Henry, we can make a snowman too.

Yes, look at all the snow.

He's a wonderful snowman.

Yes, but he must have a hat.

There's a hat in the cupboard in Dad's bedroom.

Oh, good!

Now he's got a hat.

And a *pipe*. He's a fine snowman now.

Who's got my hat? And where's my pipe?

DRAW A MAN

Let's have a *drawing* championship
with *dice*:

First you must *throw* a 6 for his body.
Then you must throw a 5 for his head.
With a 4 you can draw an arm;
with a 3 you can give him a hand,
with a 2 you give him a foot, and with a
1 you give him a leg.
But you must give him two legs,
two arms, two hands and two feet.

Now let's make his face.
You must throw a 5 for his mouth and
a 4 for his nose.
With a 3 you can give him an eye.
With a 2 give him an ear and with
a 1 give him his hair.

And now his clothes:
With a 6 you give him a pair of trousers.
With a 5 he gets his jacket, and with
a 4 he gets his *tie*. You must throw a 3 for
a shoe and a 2 for his hat.
With a 1 you can give him an umbrella.

Has your man got everything?
Who is first? Who wins?

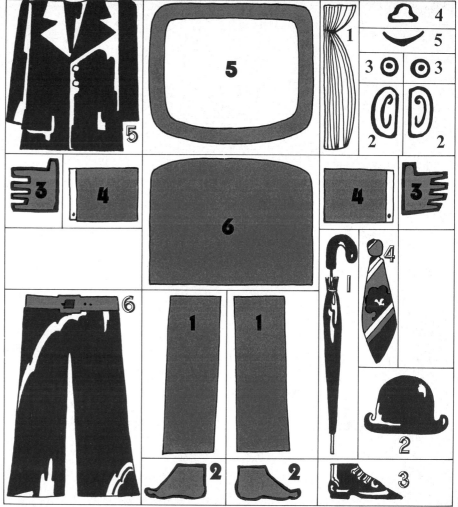

THE ROBOT

The Browns have got a *robot*. He can walk with his legs and work with his hands. He has not got a mouth, but he can write words and sentences on a piece of paper. He is very *useful* and does a lot of work for the Browns. He cleans the rooms for Mrs Brown, he helps in the garden, every Saturday he washes Mr Brown's car, and sometimes he does Fred's and Peggy's *homework*.

But sometimes he is out of order, and then he does a lot of funny things.

Today he is going shopping for Mrs Brown. In the shop he gives Miss Baker, the shop-assistant, his shopping list. Miss Baker reads:

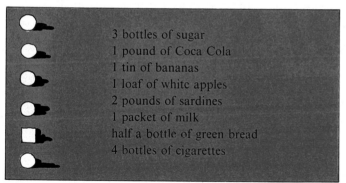

3 bottles of sugar
1 pound of Coca Cola
1 tin of bananas
1 loaf of white apples
2 pounds of sardines
1 packet of milk
half a bottle of green bread
4 bottles of cigarettes

Miss Baker looks at the list and looks at the robot.
There must be something wrong with him. Can you help her and write down the list for her?

PEGGY'S BIRTHDAY PARTY

"Hooray! It's March 3rd. It's my birthday. I'm thirteen today.
I'm having a birthday *party* this afternoon. All my
friends are coming: Sally's already here. Now we're waiting
for Anne, Betty and Susan. Ah, here they are."

Anne: ⎫
Betty: ⎬ Happy birthday, Peggy.
Susan: ⎭

Peggy: Thank you. Oh, presents! Thank you very much.
Now come in, please. Sally's already here.

Anne: Is it nice to be thirteen?
Peggy: Oh yes, it is. I'm a *teenager* now. And it's nice to
have a birthday. I've got a lot of presents.
I must open them now.
Betty: Good *idea*!

Susan: What's in this box, Peggy?
Peggy: Let's see. Oh, look, it's a scarf from *Aunt* Linda.
Anne: Isn't that nice?
Sally: And what's in this red paper?
Susan: Stop, Sally! Let Peggy open it.
Peggy: Let me see. Oh, it's a record from Betty.
What a surprise! Thank you very much, Betty.
Mother: Peggy, Peggy!

Peggy: Oh, listen! Tea's ready. We can open the other presents after tea.
Sally: Good, I'm hungry!
Anne: Mmm, these sandwiches are wonderful.
Susan: Yes, they are. Can I have an *egg* sandwich, please?
Peggy: Here you are, Susan. A cup of tea, Betty?
Betty: No, thanks. A glass of lemonade for me, please.
Peggy: And here's the birthday cake. Who *wants* a piece?
Betty: You must *blow out* the *candles* first.
Peggy: All right.

Anne: Let me count: two, four, six, eight ...
thirteen candles! Can you blow them all out *at once*?
Sally: Can we help you, Peggy?
Peggy: No, thank you. Watch! One, two, three ... Whoooo!
Susan: Very good! All thirteen at once.
Peggy: Now you can all have a piece of cake.
Anne: And now let's sing "Happy birthday to you".
Betty: This is a wonderful party. When's the next birthday?

Hap-py birth-day to you! Hap-py birth-day to you!
Hap-py birth-day, dear Peg-gy. Hap-py birth-day to you!

FRED AND PEGGY
GO SHOPPING

Fred: I must buy a new pullover.

Peggy: But you've got a lot of pullovers.

Fred: No, I haven't. Not nice pullovers.

Peggy: Oh all right. Here's a shop, then.

Assistant: Good morning. Can I help you?

Fred: Good morning. Can I look at some pullovers, please?

Assistant: What *size* are you?

Fred: Thirty-two.

Peggy: No, you aren't. You're a thirty-four.

Assistant: The thirty-fours are over here.

Peggy: Oh, that's a nice pullover.

Fred: No, it isn't. It's pink. Pink pullovers are for girls. I'm a boy. Look, this green pullover's nice. I *like* green.

Peggy: Yes, I like green, too. But it's not very warm. Look, it's too thin.

Assistant: We've got some warm pullovers over here.

Fred: Oh yes. I like this red pullover. But it's a size thirty-two.

Assistant: Here's a thirty-four. It's £8.10.

Peggy: £8.10! That's expensive!

Fred: It's very nice …

Peggy: … but very expensive.

Fred: Well, it's my money, and I like it.

COME TO THE CIRCUS

Tom and his friend Chris have got three tickets for the *circus*. Here they are telephoning a friend.

Peggy: 449 7635. Hello?
Tom: Hello, Peggy. This is Tom.
Peggy: Oh, hello, Tom. How are you?
Tom: I'm O.K., thank you.
       How are you?
Peggy: Fine, thanks.

Tom: Peggy, there's a circus *in town*.
       I've got three tickets for this afternoon. Chris is coming.
       Do you want to come, too?
Peggy: Oh yes, please. But I must ask Mother first.
       Wait a moment, please.
Tom: All right.
Peggy: Tom, it's O.K. I can come.
       Where is the circus?

Tom: It's in the park behind the station. Let's *meet* at the bus stop in front of the shopping centre.
Peggy: Ah yes, I know … What time?
Tom: Well, the circus begins at 4.
       Let's say at half past three.
Peggy: All right. 'Bye, Tom.
Tom: 'Bye, Peggy.

Chris: Oh look! What a funny man!
Peggy: Who is he?
Tom: He's *Bobo*, the *clown*.
Peggy: Look at his shoes!
　　　Aren't they big?
Chris: And his face! I like his nose.
Tom: What's he doing now? I can't see.
Chris: He's playing the trumpet.
Peggy: Oh, he can't play, listen.
　　　It's all wrong.
Tom: Look – he wants to run,
　　　but his trousers are too long.
Peggy: Oh, isn't he funny!
　　　What's *next*?

Tom, Peggy and Chris are at the circus.
Tom: Here are the *horses*.
　　　Three white and three black.
Peggy: I like the white horses.
Chris: Do you?
　　　I like the black horses.
Tom: I like them all.
　　　Look, they can walk on two legs.
Chris: And now they're *dancing*
　　　to the music.
Peggy: Oh, now it's over.
　　　They're going out. What a *pity!*

Tom: The elephants.
　　　Look, there they are.
Chris: Oh, aren't there a lot!
Peggy: And they're so big!
Tom: How many are there?
Peggy: Let's see … seven.
Chris: No, nine – look,
　　　two more are coming.
Peggy: Oh yes.
　　　And one is a *baby* elephant.
Tom: That must be *Mumbo* with
　　　his mother.
Chris: Look, now all the elephants
　　　are standing on two legs.
Peggy: I like elephants.
　　　Isn't this a wonderful circus.

25

A FANTASTIC STORY

Every morning at 7.45 I drive to work. Every morning I must slow down at the traffic lights in Old Street. Often the lights are red and I must stop and wait for the cars from New Street.

Today is Monday and the *traffic* is very bad this morning. Men are hurrying to work, children are running to school. Now the lights in Old Street are green, but the cars cannot go. The cars from New Street are still standing there.

Now the lights are yellow, and now they are red again. Yellow, green, yellow, red, yellow, green ... The cars cannot go. Some drivers begin to *shout*. They are late for work. But listen, what is that? All the people are looking *up*. One of the cars is flying, it is flying like a *helicopter!* What a surprise! The driver – or is it the pilot now? – is flying *over* the streets. For him Monday morning traffic is no *problem!*

27

HOLIDAYS ARE HERE AGAIN

For many people a "holiday" must be a seaside holiday.
They want miles of sandy beach, rocks for diving, nice warm
water for swimming, a good hotel – not too expensive –,
a lot of *sunshine* and not too many people there.
But what they often get is a beach *so* full of people
that they must ask their way to the water.
Some people have other ideas of a wonderful holiday:
Here is Peter with his friends. They are camping in the Lake
District. They always go to a camping site *near* the big lakes.
They can swim and *fish* there and walk in the mountains, too.
Now they are cooking dinner. They are very hungry after
a long day.

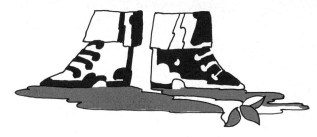

Susan and Peggy are on holiday in Wales. They are having a walking holiday. Every day they walk more than 20 miles. They sleep in *youth hostels*. These are very cheap and they *meet* a lot of other young people there.

Susan: Gosh! I'm *tired*. Is it *far* to the hostel?

Peggy: No, it isn't. Look, it's down there.
Let's go and get something to drink.

Susan: And sit down. Oh my feet!

Here is the *Winter* family: Father, Mother and eight children. They like *fishing*. Every year they go to Scotland. Mr Winter says: "Scotland's ideal for fishing. There are a lot of lonely blue lakes and small *streams* full of fish. We get up at five o'clock every morning."

Only one of the family does not fish. That is Robert. He is one year old.

Tom & Henry

Hooray! The summer holidays are here.

A camping holiday. What a good idea.

Look at the map. That's a *field* there. We can *camp* there.

This is a nice field. We can eat now and then we can sleep.

Tom, get up! There's a *storm*.

Oh no! Where's our *tent*?

What a terrible storm this morning!

But it's nice here.

Henry, Henry! Look, there's a *cow* in the tent.

This is a terrible holiday. First a storm and then a cow in the tent.

Tom, I'm *tired*. Let's stop now.

All right, Henry. I can see a nice field over there. Let's stay there.

Oh no!

PUZZLE PAGE

I haven't got a brother or a sister, but this boy's father is my father's son.

WHO IS HE?

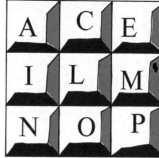

A	C	E
I	L	M
N	O	P

These are the 9 letters of an English word. *Which* word is it? You can make 20 other English words with these letters. Write them down.

Can you write these numbers so that they always make 15 – across, down or *diagonally*?

1	2	3
4	5	6
7	8	9

(Answers on page 33.)

Can you read this sentence:
The *last* letter of every word is the first letter of the next word.

CHRI S END S USA N INETEE N E W HIT E LEPHANTS

Alphabetical Word List

address	əˈdres	Adresse
at once	ət ˈwʌns	auf einmal
Aunt Linda	ɑːnt ˈlində	Tante Linda
baby	ˈbeibi	Baby
Baker	ˈbeikə	Familienname
Betty	ˈbeti	Mädchenname
blow out	ˈbləu ˈaut	ausblasen
Bob	bɔb	Jungenname
Bobo	ˈbəubəu	Name des Clowns
break	breik	Pause
Brown	braun	Familienname
Bush Street	ˈbuʃ striːt	Busch Straße
camp	kæmp	zelten
candle	ˈkændl	Kerze
chips	tʃips	Pommes frites
Chris	kris	Jungenname
Christmas	ˈkrisməs	Weihnachten
circus	ˈsəːkəs	Zirkus
clown	klaun	Clown, dummer August
collecting	kəˈlektiŋ	Sammeln
colour it!	ˈkʌlər_it	male es an!
comic	ˈkɔmik	Comic, Bildgeschichte
cow	kau	Kuh
dance	dɑːns	tanzen
diagonally	daiˈægənəli	diagonal
dice	dais	Würfel
draw! drawing	drɔː ˈdrɔːiŋ	zeichne! Zeichnen
egg	eg	Ei
everywhere	ˈevriwɛə	überall
fantastic	fænˈtæstik	fantastisch
far	fɑː	weit
field	fiːld	Feld, Acker
fish	fiʃ	fischen
flour	ˈflauə	Mehl
gosh!	gɔʃ	puh! (Ausruf)
hard	hɑːd	hart
helicopter	ˈhelikɔptə	Hubschrauber
Henry	ˈhenri	Jungenname
hobby	ˈhɔbi	Hobby, Steckenpferd
holidays	ˈhɔlədiz	Ferien
homework	ˈhəumwəːk	Hausaufgaben
hooray!	huˈrei	hurra!
horse	ˈhɔːs	Pferd
idea	aiˈdiə	Idee
John	dʒɔn	Jungenname
the last	ˈlɑːst	der letzte
he likes	ˈlaiks	er mag gern
magic square	ˈmædʒik ˈskwɛə	magisches Quadrat
meet	miːt	treffen
Miss	mis	Fräulein
Mumbo	ˈmʌmbəu	Elefantenname
music	ˈmjuːzik	Musik
near	niə	nahe bei
what's next?	wɔts ˈnekst	was kommt als nächstes?
over	ˈɔuvə	über
party	ˈpɑːti	Party, Einladung
Peggy	ˈpegi	Mädchenname
pipe	paip	Pfeife
what a pity!	ˈwɔt ə ˈpiti	wie schade!
problem	ˈprɔbləm	Problem
he is putting on	ˈputiŋ ˈɔn	er zieht … an
tennis racket	ˈtenis ˈrækit	Tennisschläger
she is right	ˈrait	sie hat recht
robot	ˈrəubɔt	Roboter

see	si:	sehen
shout	ʃaut	schreien
size	saiz	Größe (von Kleidung)
snowman	'snəumæn	Schneemann
so ... that	'səu 'ðæt	so ..., daß
Steve	sti:v	Jungenname
storm	stɔ:m	Sturm
stream	stri:m	Bach
street	stri:t	Straße
sunny, sunshine	'sʌni 'sʌnʃain	sonnig, Sonnenschein
Susan	'su:zn	Mädchenname
swimming	'swimiŋ	Schwimmen
teenager	'ti:neidʒə	Teenager
tell me!	'tel mi	sagt mir!
tent	tent	Zelt
throw	θrəu	werfen
tie	tai	Krawatte
(no) time for	(nəu)'taim fə	(keine) Zeit für
(no) time to	(nəu)'taim tə	(keine) Zeit zu
tired	'taiəd	müde
in town	in 'taun	in der Stadt
traffic	'træfik	Verkehr
understand	ʌndə'stænd	verstehen
up	ʌp	auf, nach oben
useful	'ju:sful	nützlich
are waiting for	'weitiŋ fə	warten auf
want	wɔnt	will, möchte
water	'wɔ:tə	Wasser
Wembley	'wembli	Vorort von London
which	witʃ	welches
Winter	'wintə	Familienname
youth hostel	'ju:θ 'hɔstl	Jugendherberge

Answers to Puzzles

Who is he?   His son.

Magic squares: Policeman

can	man	name	pencil
cap	map	nice	piano
clean	meal	on	plan
come	men	one	plane
lamp	mile	open	police

2	9	4
7	5	3
6	1	8

Can you read this sentence?

CHRIS SENDS SUSAN
NINETEEN NEW WHITE ELEPHANTS.

Read and Play

9783125711303.3

Stage Readers – Elementarstufe 1

Klettbuch 57111   All in a Day
Klettbuch 57112   Anything to Declare?
Klettbuch 57113   Read and Play

ISBN 3-12-**57113** 0-4